RECORDED VERSIONS
GUITAR

AUTHENTIC TRANSCRIPTIONS
WITH NOTES AND TABLATURE

SLAYER

GUITAR COLLECTION

Cover photo by Marty Temme

ISBN 978-1-4234-0467-5

HAL•LEONARD®
CORPORATION

7777 W. BLUEMOUND RD. P.O. BOX 13819 MILWAUKEE, WI 53213

Visit Hal Leonard Online at
www.halleonard.com

Angel of Death

Words and Music by Jeff Hanneman

1. Ausch - witz, the mean-ing of pain,— the why that I want— you to die.—

Slow death, im - mense de - cay,— show-ers that cleanse— you of your life.

Forced in like cat-tle, you run,— stripped of your life's worth.—

Hu-man mice   for the an-gel of death.__   Four hun-dred thou-sand more to die.

Chorus
w/Rhy. Figs. 1 & 1A (both 2 times)

An-gel of death,__

mon-arch to the king-dom of the dead.   2. Sa-

2nd Verse
w/Rhy. Fig. 2 (2 times)

dis-tic   sur-geon of de-mise,   sa-dist of the no-blest blood.__   De-

stroy-ing   with-out mer-cy__   to ben-e-fit the Ar-y-an race.__

Sur-ger-y   with no an-es-the-sia.   Feel the knife pierce you in-tense-ly.   In-

fe-ri-or,   no use__ to man-kind.   Strapped down,   scream-ing out to   die.__

Chorus
w/Rhy. Figs. 1 (3 times) & 1A (2 times)

__   An-gel of death,__

mon-arch to the king-dom of the dead.

Black Magic

Words and Music by Jeff Hanneman and Kerry King

Death takes my hand ____ and cap - tures my soul.

Faster ♩ = 186
Guitar solo II
w/1st half of Rhy. Fig. 1 (4 times)

*pick slide

*Depress stgs. against fretboard near the nut w/edge of pick
and move towards bridge.

*Descend back towards nut.

*Pull bar up.

(Gtr. IV out)

Chemical Warfare

Words and Music by Jeff Hanneman and Kerry King

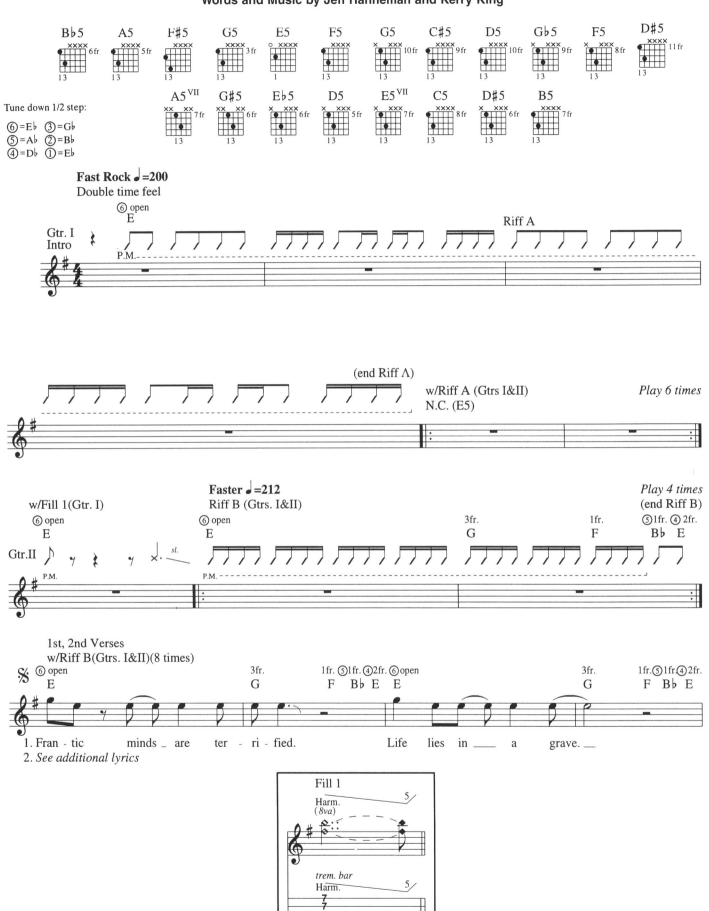

Si - lent death rides high _ a - bove _ on wings of rev - e - la - tion.

Mul - ti - death from chem - i - cals. Ar - ro - gance as won. _ An -

ni - hi - la - tion must _ be swift. De - stroy with - out de - struc - tion.

Chorus
Rhy. Fig. 1
(Gtrs. I&II)

Gods of the throne must be watch-ing from hell, wait-ing the mass gen - o - cide. _

Sol - diers de - feat - ed by death from a smell. Bod - ies lie dor-mant, no life. _

Ris - ing now souls on the land where they fell. De - mons not read - y to die. _

2nd time to Coda I   *3rd time to Coda II*

Noth - ing to see where the sleep-ing souls _ lie. _____

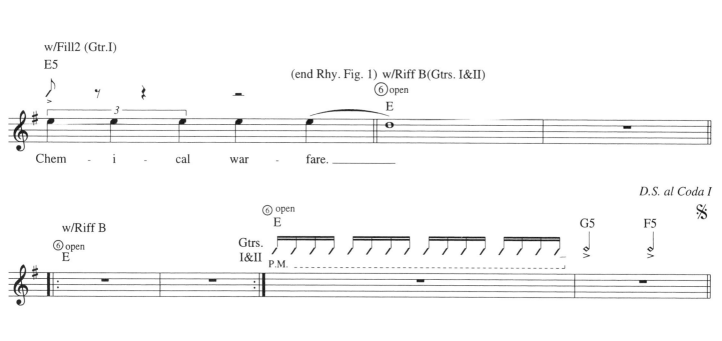

Chem - i - cal war - fare. _____

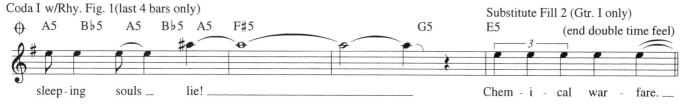

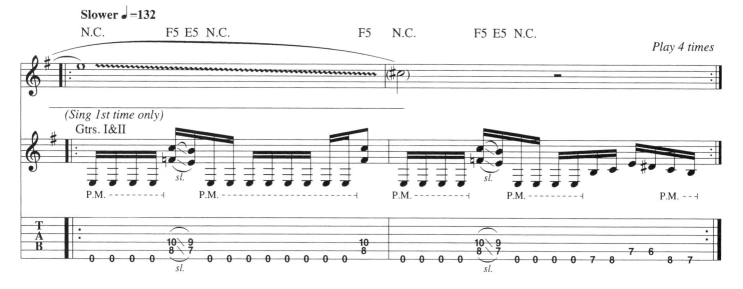

sleep-ing souls _ lie! _____

Chem - i - cal war - fare. _

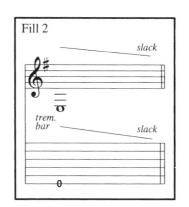

Fill 2

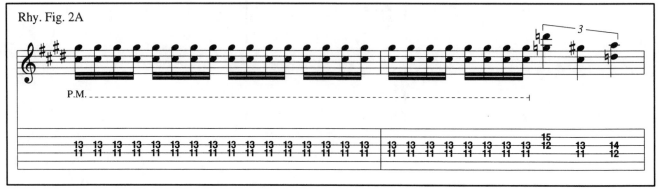

Guitar solo I
w/Rhy. Fig. 2(Gtrs. I&II)(3¹/₂ times)

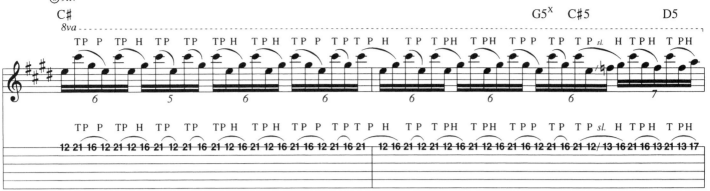

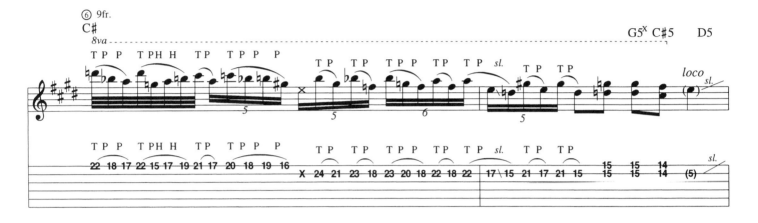

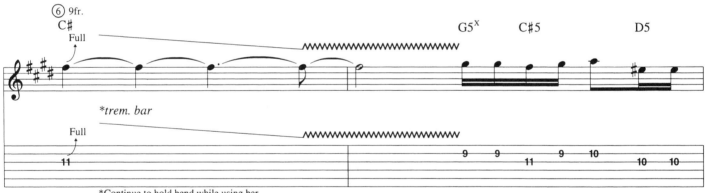

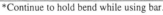

*Continue to hold bend while using bar.

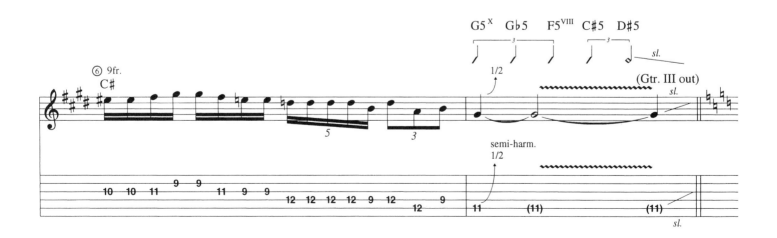

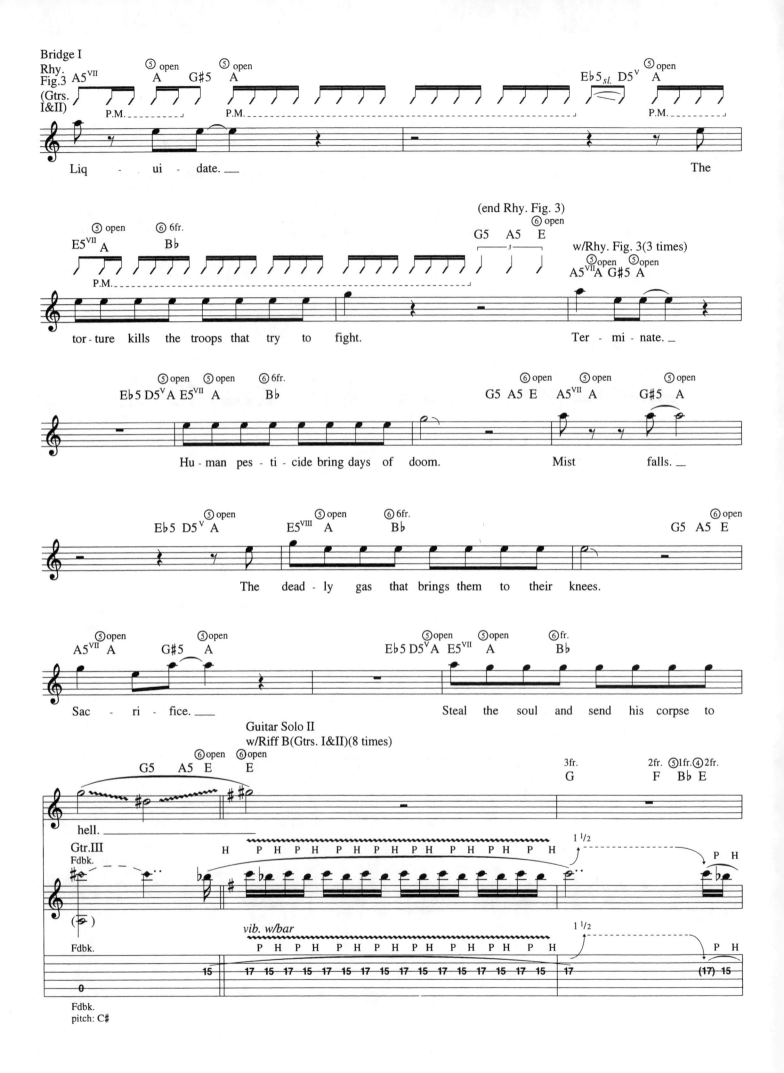

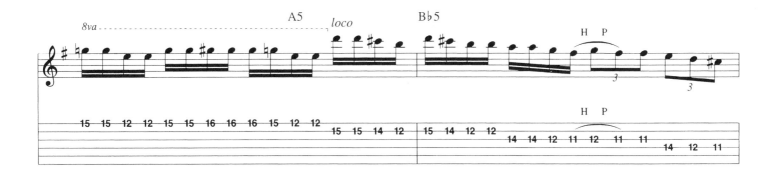

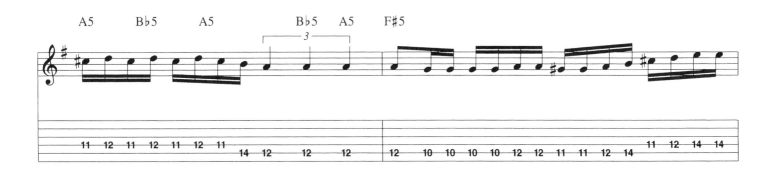

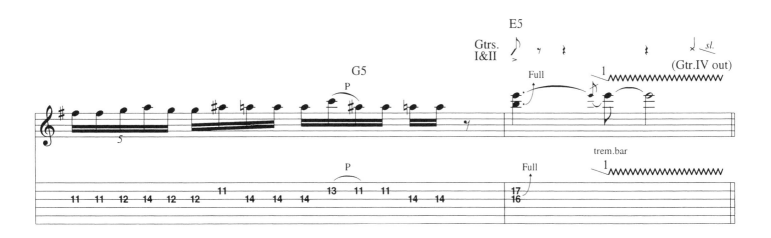

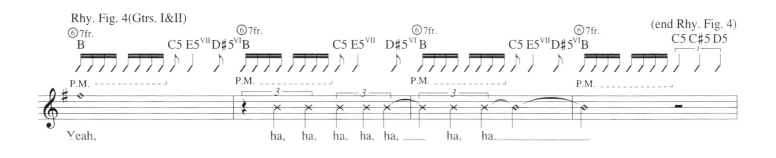

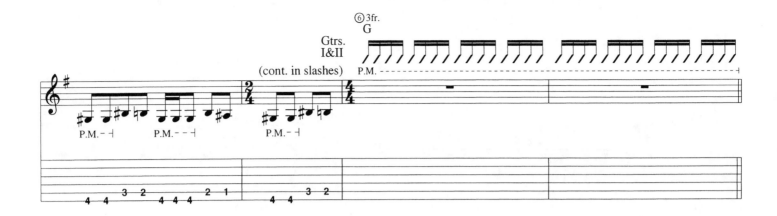

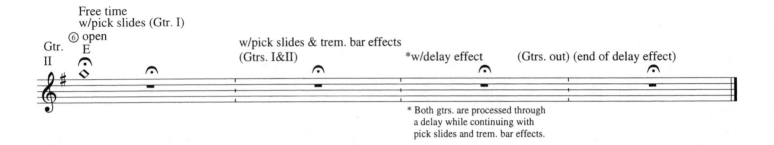

* Both gtrs. are processed through
a delay while continuing with
pick slides and trem. bar effects.

Additional Lyrics

2. Artificial fuckin' peace.
   Line up in death row.
   Generals in their slow defeat
   Diminish from this hell.
   The lords of hell await.
   Dogs of war are helpless prey
   To immortality. *(To Chorus)*

Dead Skin Mask

Words and Music by Jeff Hanneman and Tom Araya

Tune down ½ step:
⑥ = E♭ ③ = G♭
⑤ = A♭ ② = B♭
④ = D♭ ① = E♭

Moderately ♩ = 109

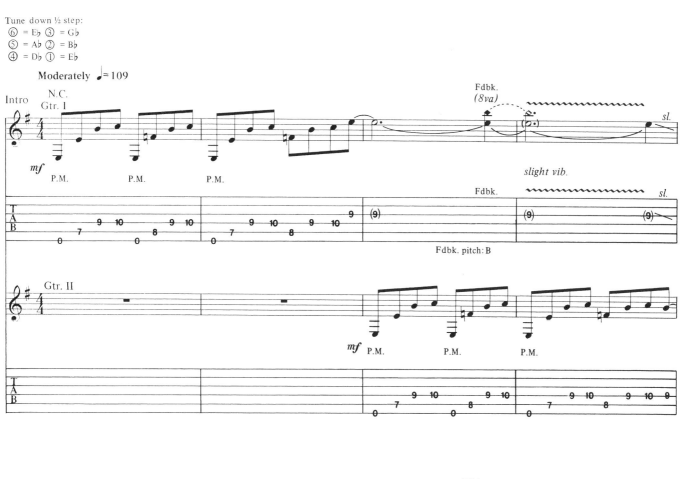

(Spoken:) How I've waited for you to come.   I've been here all alone.   Now that you've

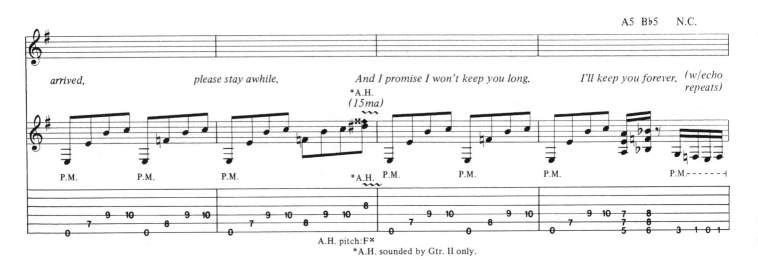

arrived,   please stay awhile.   And I promise I won't keep you long.   I'll keep you forever.   (w/echo repeats)

In the depths of a mind in - sane fan - ta - sy and re - al - i - ty are the same.

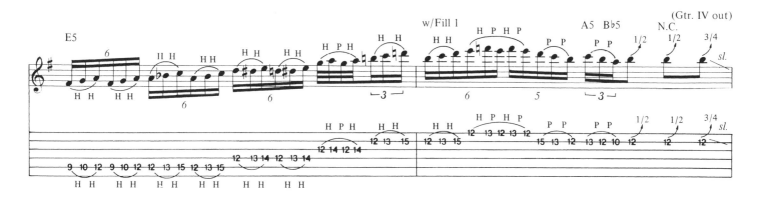

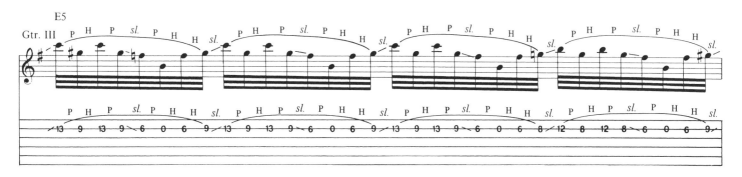

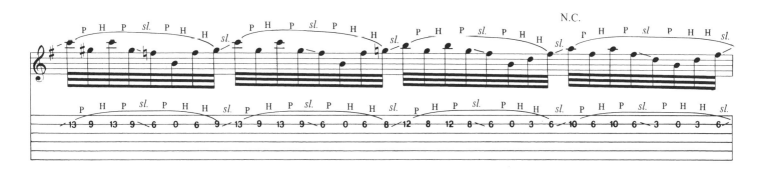

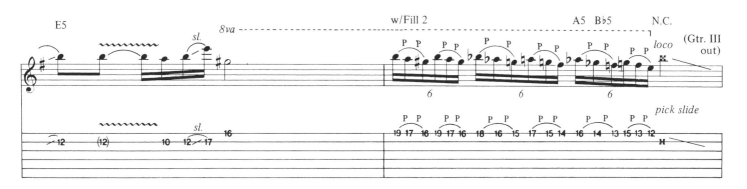

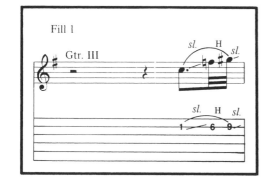

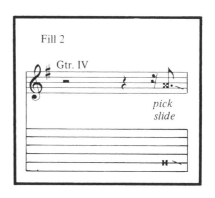

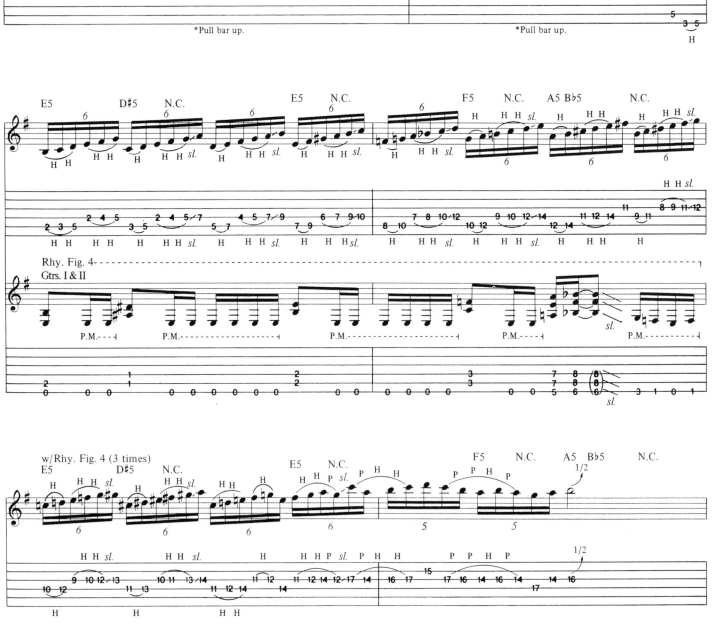

Recitation

Child's voice:
Hello?
Hello, Mr. Gein.
Mr. Gein?
Let me outta here, Mr. Gein.
Mr. Gein, I don't wanna play anymore, Mr. Gein.
Mr. Gein, it's not any fun anymore.
I don't wanna play in here, Mr. Gein.
Mr. Gein?
I want outta here, Mr. Gein.
Let me out now!

Dittohead

Words and Music by Kerry King

le - gal sys - tem has__ no spine, it's cor - rod - ing from in - side, slap your hand, you'll do no time.

Re - al - i - ty on__ va - ca - tion, all a - cross a blind - ed na - tion,

men - tal - ly un - der se - da - tion. An - y - one can be set free on a tech - ni - cal - i - ty, ex-

plain the law a - gain__ to me.

gret!__

Noth - ing to re -

Un - im - pos - ing pol - i - cy,__

no en - forc - ing min - is - try.__ Gap - ing with ju - di - cial flaws,__ watch a fad - ing

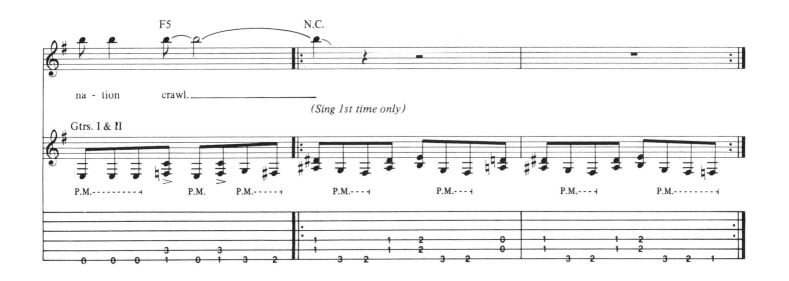

na - tion   crawl._____

(Sing 1st time only)

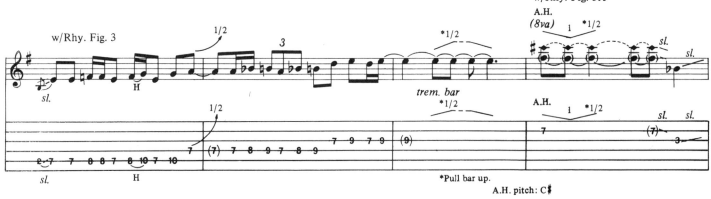

Rhy. Fig. 3B (Gtrs. I & II)

Clash - ing with the pub - lic's frame,___ I'm the one that's

placed in fame. Leg - is - la - ture sets the stage, so - cial slaves caught in my rage.___

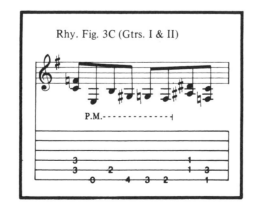

Rhy. Fig. 3C (Gtrs. I & II)

Additional Lyrics

2. Here in 1994
Things are different than before,
Violence is what we adore.
Invitation to the game,
Guns and blades and media fame,
Every day more of the same.
Murder, mayhem, anarchy
Now are all done legally,
Mastermind your killing spree.
Unafraid of punishment,
With a passive government
There's nothing for you to regret.

Divine Intervention

Words and Music by Jeff Hanneman, Tom Araya, Kerry King and Paul Bostaph

w/Rhy. Fig. 2 (3 times)

Why are they haunt-ing me?___ I can-not___ look at___ God's face.

Par - a - lyz - ing bril - liant light.___ Try - ing to run.___

1st time w/Fill 1

2nd time to Coda I;
3rd time to Coda II

Want to scream, but can - not speak.___ I can-not___ look at___ God's face.

Fill 1 (Gtr. VI)

51

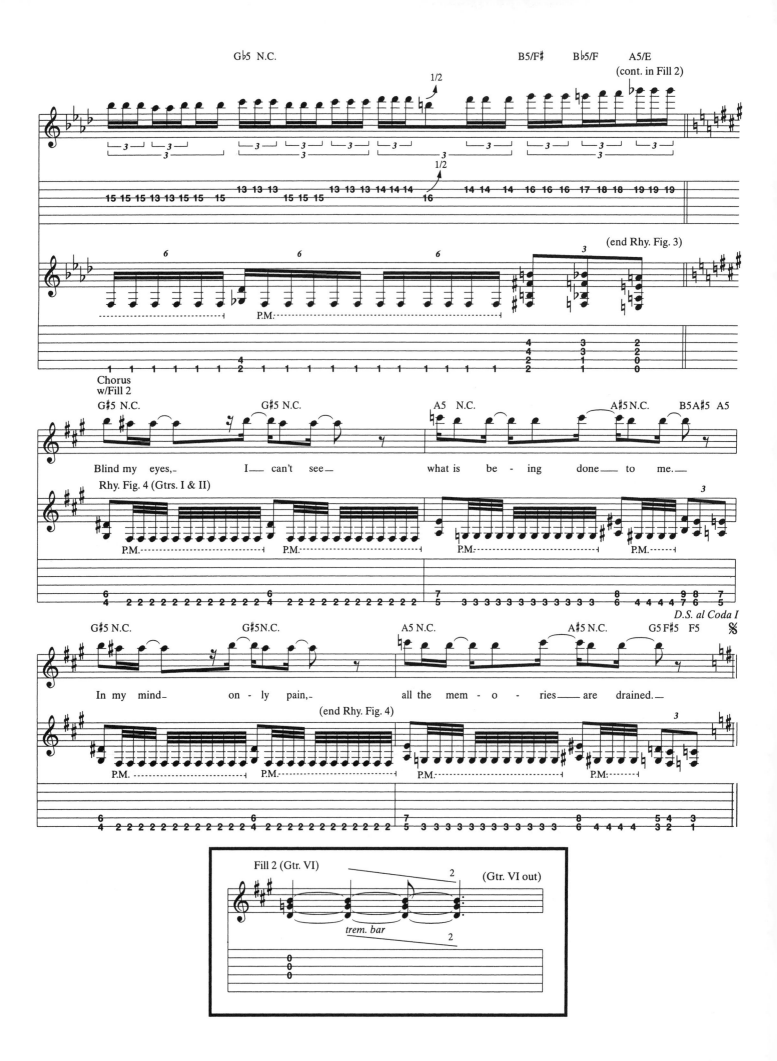

54

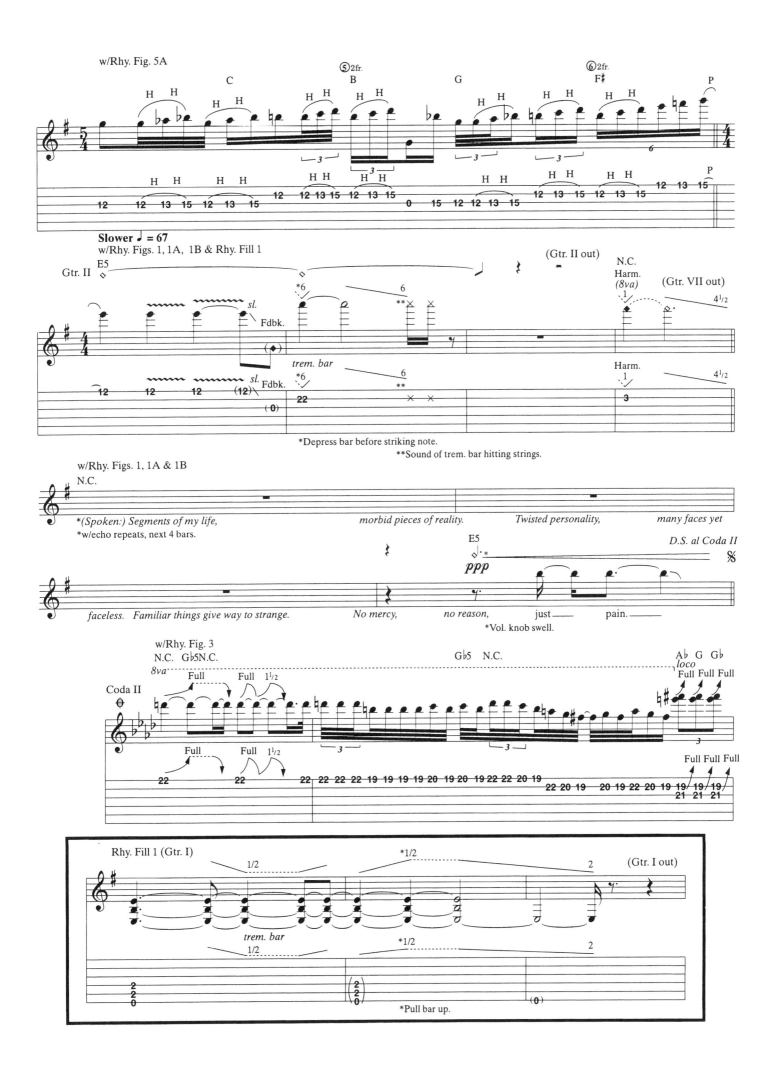

*Depress bar before striking note.

**Sound of trem. bar hitting strings.

*(Spoken:) Segments of my life,   morbid pieces of reality.   Twisted personality,   many faces yet

*w/echo repeats, next 4 bars.

faceless.   Familiar things give way to strange.   No mercy,   no reason,   just___ pain.___

*Vol. knob swell.

*Pull bar up.

*When P.M. is indicated play lowest note of chord only, next 4 bars only.

Additional Lyrics

2. Victimized specimen.
   Deathless torture.
   Void with no mercy.
   Black shroud blinds those who see.
   Violated!
   Naked, before you I stand.
   Shattered shrine of flesh and bone.
   God's piercing through my soul. *(To Coda I)*

3. Fatal subconscious control.
   Threshold of pain unfolds.
   Transfixed martyr saving race.
   Who am I to judge thy grace?
   Awaken in a web like hell.
   How did I reach this place?
   Why are they haunting me?
   I cannot look at God's face. *(To Coda II)*

Hell Awaits

Words and Music by Jeff Hanneman and Kerry King

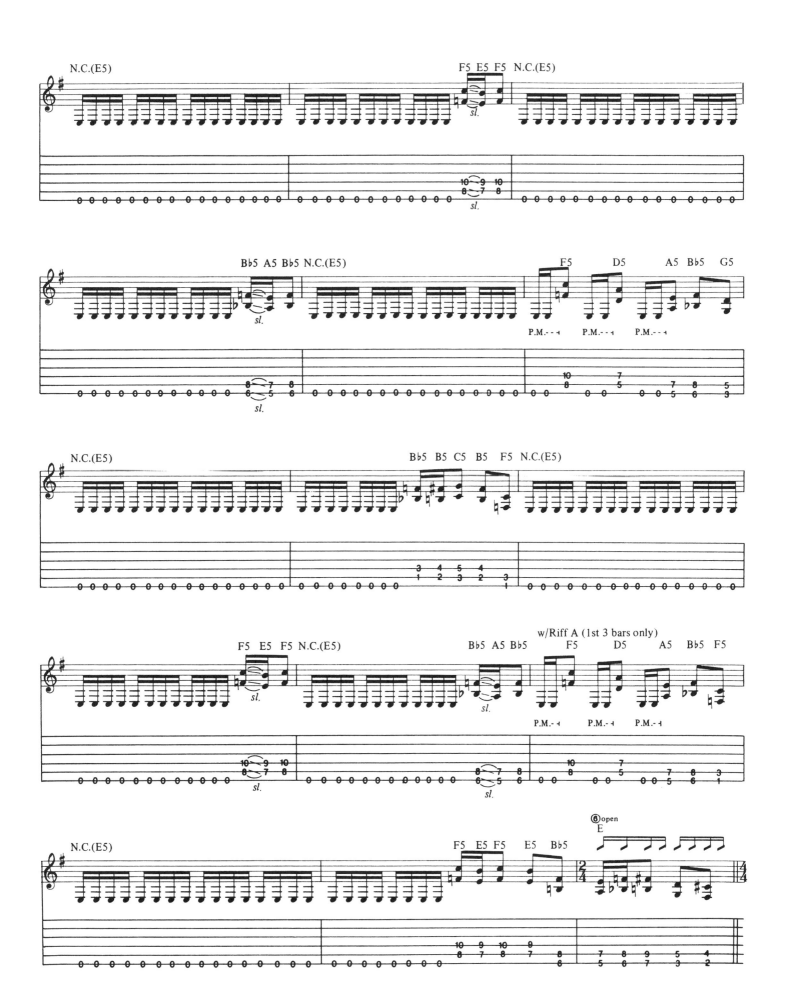

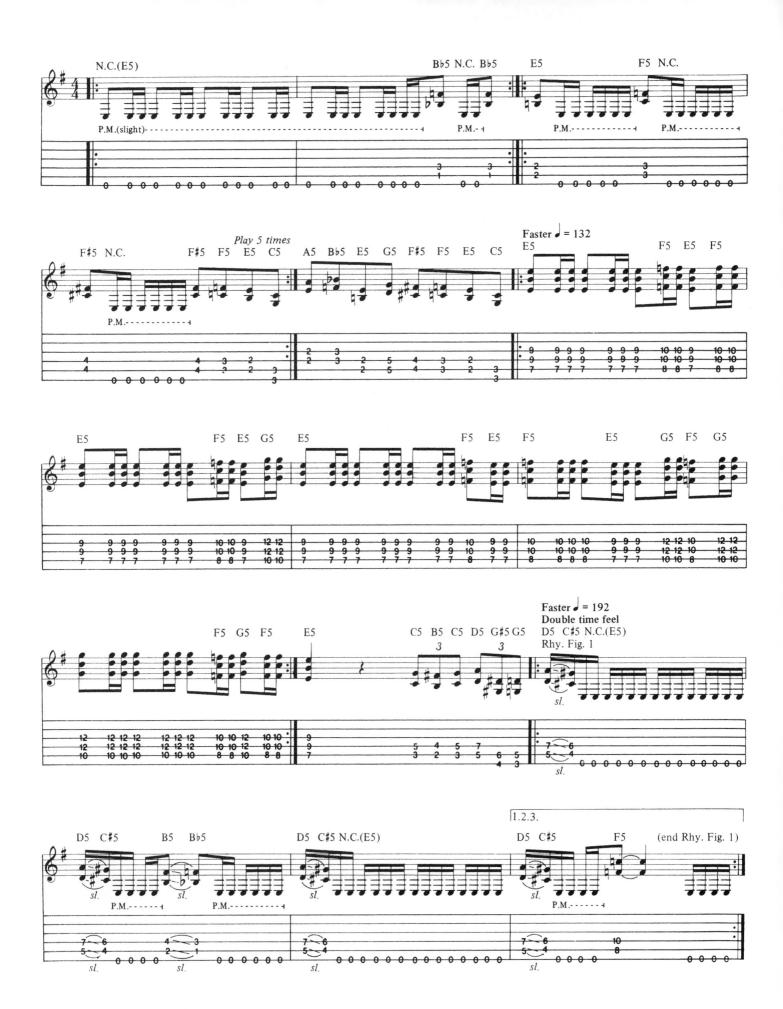

Je - sus knows your soul can - not be saved.
Sa - tan - ic laws pre - vail, your life is

1. Cru - ci - fy___ the so called Lord, he soon shall fall to me.___ Your souls are damned, your god has fell to
2. Sac - ri - fice___ the lives of all I know, they soon shall die.___ Their souls are damned. to rot in hell and

slave for me e - ter - nal - ly.
keep the fire grow - ing deep in - side.

Hell a -

waits!___

2. The through.

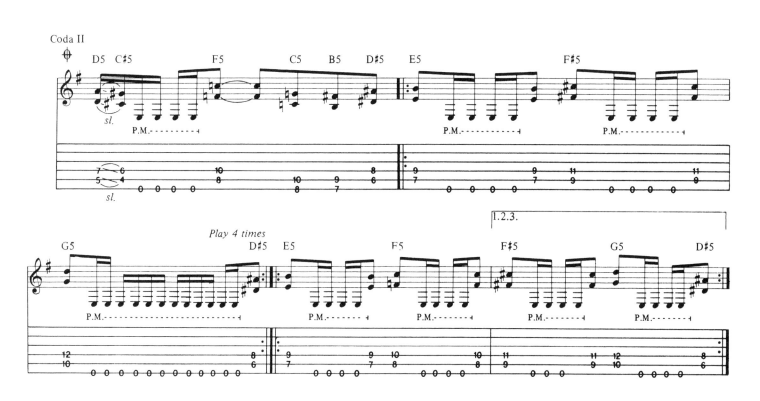

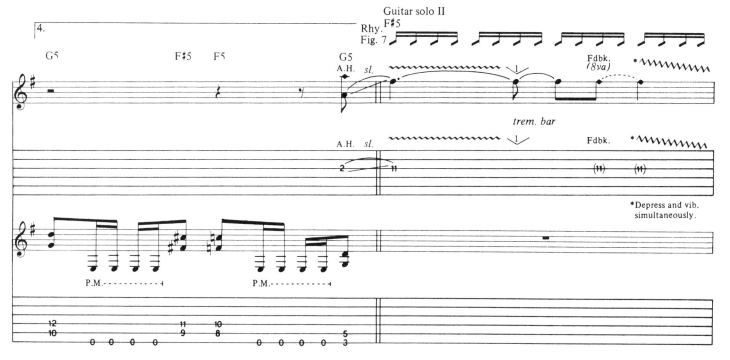

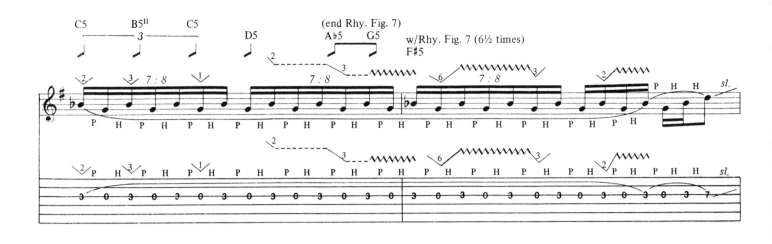

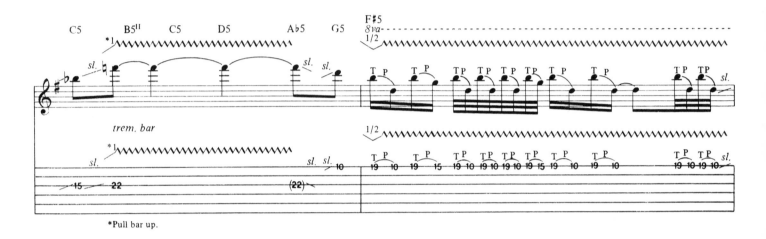

*Pull bar up.

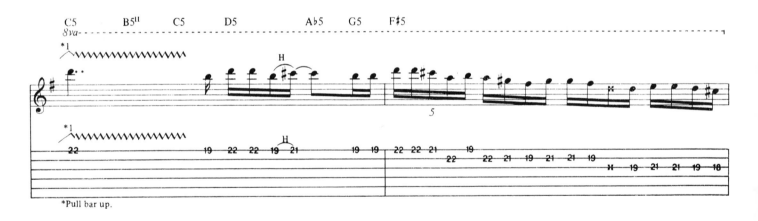

*Pull bar up.

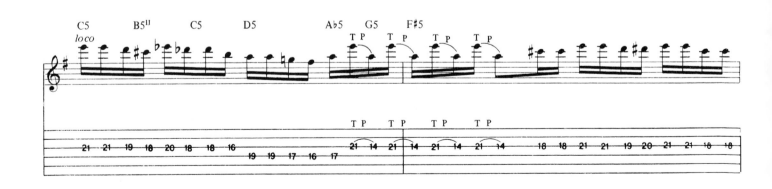

*Depress stgs. against fretboard at 12fr.
w/edge of pick and move towards nut.

*Pull bar up.

*Pull bar up.

*Pull bar up.

Additional Lyrics

2. The reaper guards the darkened gates that Satan calls his home.
Demons feed the furnace where the dead are free to roam.
Lonely children of the night, there's seven ways to go;
Each leading to the burning whole that Lucifer controls. *(To Pre-chorus)*

3. Now I have you deep inside my ever lasting grasp.
The seven bloody gates of hell is where you'll live your last.
Warriors from hell's domain will bring you to your death.
The flames of Hades burning strong, your soul shall never rest. *(To Pre-chorus)*

Mandatory Suicide

Words and Music by Jeff Hanneman, Tom Araya and Kerry King

Burn!_____
(Sing 1st time only)

2. Am - bushed by the spray of lead.___ Count the bul - let holes in your head.___
3. Holes burn deep in your chest,___ raked by ma - chine gun fire.___

Off - spring sent___ out to cry,_____ } liv - ing man - da - to - ry su - i - cide.___
Scream-ing skull sent___ out to die,_____ }

Su - i - cide._ Su - i - cide._

Recitation:

Lying, dying, screaming in pain.
Begging, pleading, bullets drop like rain.
Minds explode, pain sheers to your brain,
Radical amputation, this is insane.
Fly swatter stakes drive through your chest.
Spikes impale you as you're forced off the crest.
Soldier of misfortune, hunting with bated breath.
A vile smell, like tasting death.
Dead bodies, dying and wounded, litter the city streets.
Shattered glass, bits of clothing and human deceit.
Dying terror, blood's cheap, it's everywhere.
Mandatory suicide, massacre on the front line.

Postmortem

Words and Music by Jeff Hanneman

Segue to RAINING BLOOD

Additional Lyrics

2. Chanting lines of blind witchery
To save yourself from extinction.
Wanting to die is your reason to live.
New life born from the oppressed.
Taste your blood as it tricks through the air.
Another casualty beyond the shadows you fall.
Losing ground, the fate you feel it draws near.
Fatality, reality, await the final call!

Raining Blood

Words and Music by Jeff Hanneman and Kerry King

Trapped in pur - ga - to - ry,____ a life - less ob - ject a - live.____

A - wait - ing re - pris - al,

death will be their ac - quit - tance.____ Sky is turn - ing red.____ Re -

turn to pow - er draws near. Fall in - to me,____ the sky's____

____ crim - son tears. A - bol - ish the rules____ made of stone.

Pierced from be - low,____ souls____ of my treach -'rous past.

Be - trayed by man - y now, or - na - ments drip - ping a - bove.____

*Gtr. II play two times only.

Half time feel
w/Riff A1 (2 times)

A - wait-ing   the hour of re - pris - al,   your time slips a -

Rhy.   **Slightly slower** ♩ = 180
Fig. 3
(Both E5ⁱⁱ
gtrs.)

way.

(end Rhy. Fig. 3)   *w/Rhy. Fig. 3 (4 times)   w/Riff B (6 times)
                          4   12

*Gtr. II play one time only.

Chorus
N.C.   G5   B5   N.C.   G5   B♭5 N.C.   G5   A5   N.C.   G5   F♯5

Rain - ing   blood _____ ____

Rhy. Fig. 4 (Both gtrs.)- -
P.M.- - - - -   P.M.- - - - -   P.M.- - - - -   P.M.- - - - -   sl.

```
5    9           5    8           5    7           5   4
0    0   3   7   0   0   3   6   0   0   3   5   0   0   3   2
```
sl.

w/Rhy. Fig. 4 (3 times)
N.C.   G5   B5 N.C.   G5 B♭5 N.C.   G5   A5 N.C.   G5 F♯5 N.C.   G5   B5 N.C.   G5 B♭5

from a lac - er - at - ed   sky.   Bleed - ing its   hor - ror.

(end half time feel)
N.C.   G5   A5 N.C.   G5 F♯5 N.C.   G5   B5 N.C.   G5 B♭5 N.C.   G5   A5 N.C.   G5 F♯5

Cre - at - ing my   struc - ture,   now   I   shall   reign in

Riff A1
Gtr. II
P.M.- - - -
```
                10  11  10        10   9        9   8
         9                  11              10
     0   0   0
```

Riff B
Gtr. II
P.M.   P.M.   P.M.   P.M.
```
         7  10     9        7  10     8      7  10     7      7  10  9
     0              0                0              0
```

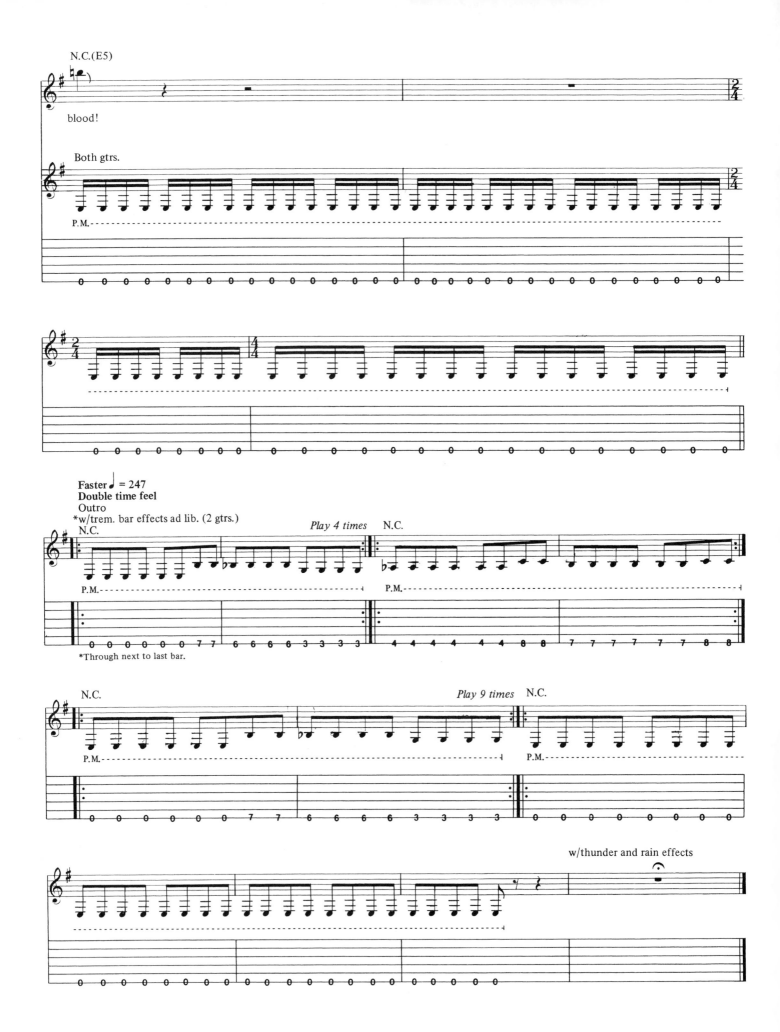

Seasons in the Abyss

Words and Music by Jeff Hanneman and Tom Araya

go — in - sane!

Additional Lyrics

2. Innate seed to watch you bleed,
   A demanding physical need.
   Desecrated, eviscerated,
   Time perpetuated. *(To Chorus)*

3. Inert flesh, a bloody tomb,
   A decorated splatter brightens the room.
   An execution, a sadist ritual,
   Mad intervals of mind residuals. *(To Chorus)*

Serenity in Murder

Words and Music by Jeff Hanneman, Tom Araya and Kerry King

South of Heaven

Words and Music by Jeff Hanneman and Tom Araya

*This note can also be produced by pulling stg. off side of neck and "fretting" stg. against pickup.

4th Verse
w/Rhy. Fig. 1

root of all e-vil is the heart of a black soul. A force that has lived all e-ter-ni-ty. The

(Gtr. I doubles Gtr. II)

nev-er end-ing search for a truth nev-er told. The loss of all hope and your dig-ni-ty.

*Vib. w/trem. bar while trilling.   **Gradually depress bar as far as possible.

w/Rhy. Fig. 5 (1st. bar only)

Fdbk. pitches: G#, E

Fdbk. pitch: D

98

Spill the Blood

Words and Music by Jeff Hanneman

1st, 2nd, 3rd Verses

1. Come walk with me through end - less time.____
2. I'll show you sights that you would not be - lieve.____
3. Spill your blood. Let it run on - to me.____

See what has been and what the fu - ture sees.____
Ex - pe - ri - ence pleas - ures thought un - ob - tained.____
Take my hand and let go of your life.____

Share the wis - dom of the old world that has passed.____
At one with e - vil that has ruled be - fore.____
Close your eyes and see what is me.____

Step in a life that's yet to be born.____
Now smell the stench of im - mor - tal - i - ty.____
Raise the chal - ice. Em - brace for - ev - er - more.____

Chorus

1.2. You spill the blood._____
3. You've spilt the blood._____

100

Eter-nal soul.
I'll have your

soul.

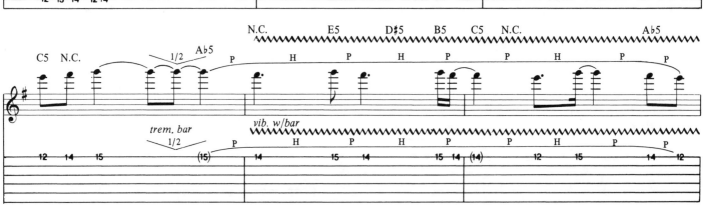

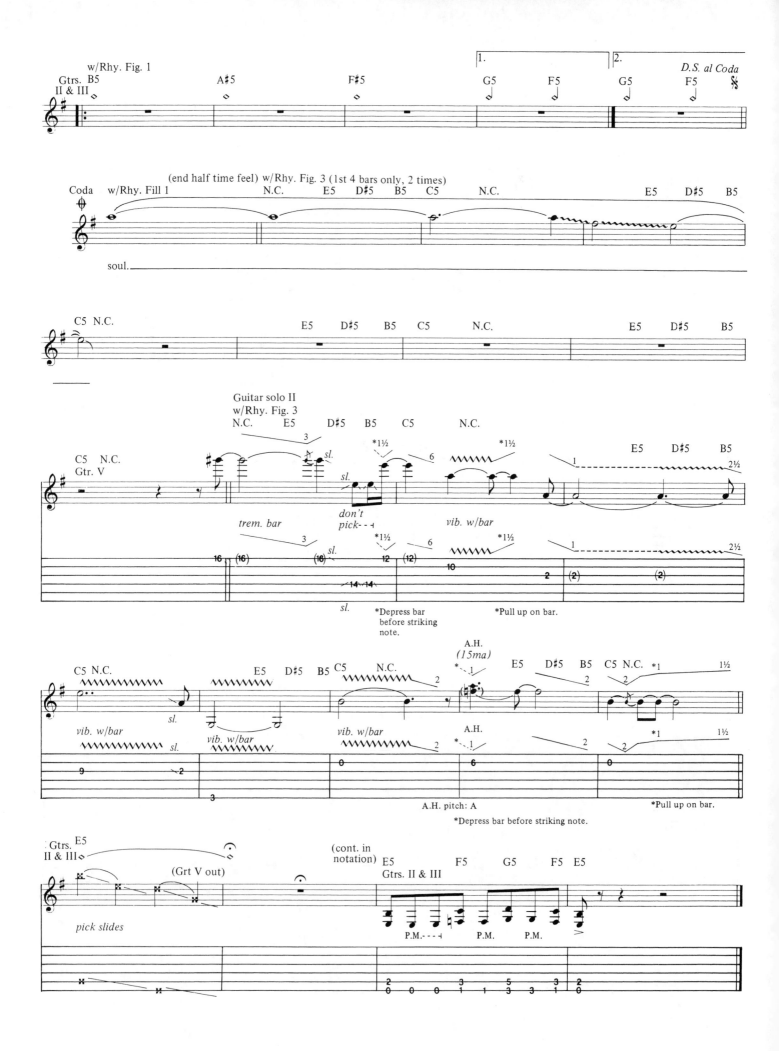

War Ensemble

Words and Music by Jeff Hanneman and Tom Araya

3rd, 4th Verses

3. Be dead fiend from a-bove when dark-ness falls.
4. Re-gime pro-phet-ic age, old in its time.

De-scend on-to my sights, your fall-en walls.
Flow-ing be-ings run on through, deep in the rhine.

Spear-head break through the lines,
Cen-ter of the web,

flanked all a-round. Sol-diers
all bat-tles scored. What is our

of at-tri-tion for-ward their ground.

Coda II

war crimes e-ra for-ev-er more!

Tempo 1

(end Rhy. Fig. 5)

w/Rhy. Fig. 5

War!

pick slide

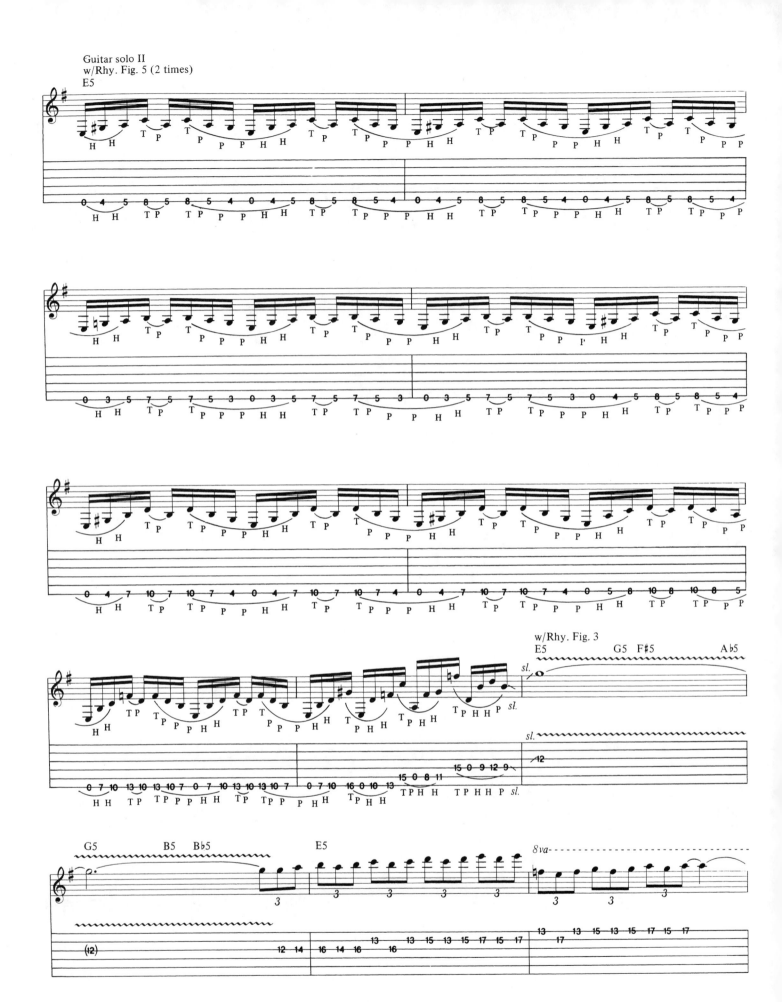

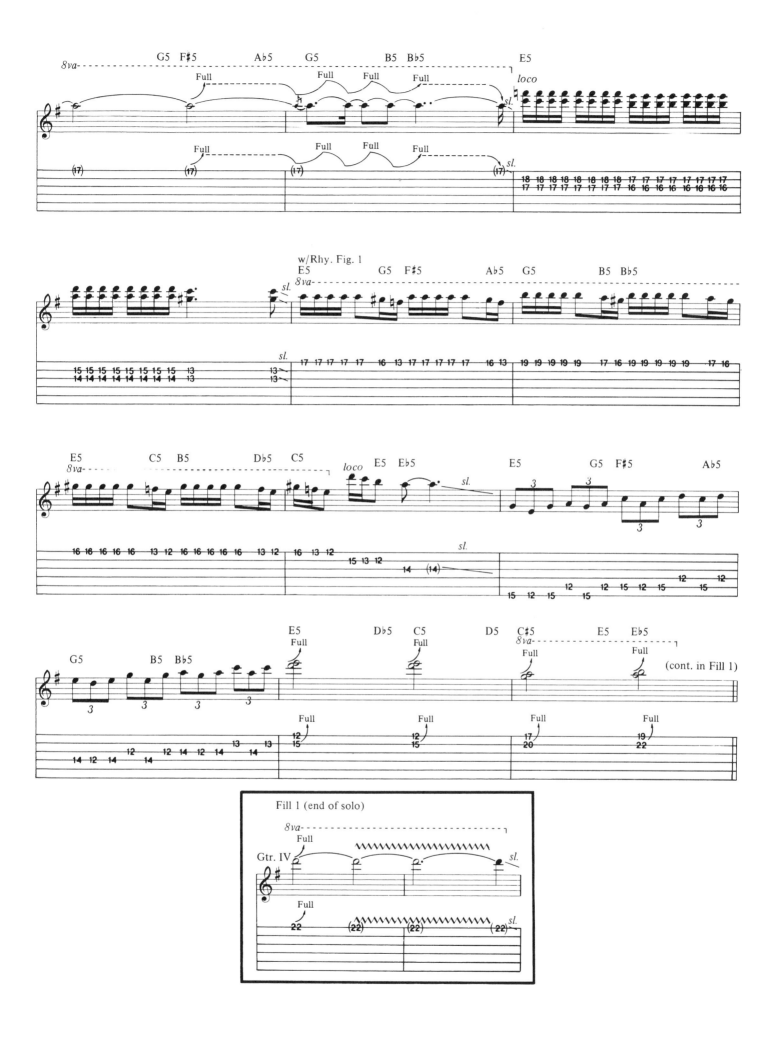